PEELING BACK THE HEART
EXPOSING THE SOUL

SALLY JO MARTINE

All content copyright © 2013 Sally Jo Martine

All rights reserved.

ISBN-13: 978-0615764665
ISBN-10: 0615764665

DEDICATION

Dedicated to Christine, for remaining courageously present – through the easy and the difficult – in a conversation spanning decades.

And to Larry, for awakening the language in my soul.

VISIT ONLINE

OneBeingHuman-sjm.com

ACKNOWLEDGMENTS

Life reveals itself as a remarkable journey where encounters – both fleeting and enduring, both pleasing and painful – regularly shape my reflections and intentions. The following are among those whose sway has been profound, and I'm ceaselessly grateful for the lessons and light: Zipprea Arbuckle, Larry Balentine, Shirli Barovich, Penny H., Gary Gill, and Christine Whitehall. Thank you for opening doors, taking my hand, and for believing in me.

1

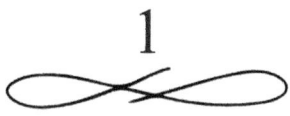

Tumbling thoughts drop like free-falling stones
on the high meadow slopes in summer.

A trail of broken images is strewn in their wake,
and their echoes rumble along the valley of my mind.

Dislodged by a mysterious hand, they gather in motion
and form a shape-shifting curtain of feelings.

Hope comes to rest at the base of an ancient cedar
and draws strength from its gnarled limbs.

Dreams skip along a ridge
and tremble before slipping into a hidden tarn.

Worries scatter, forming the rippled shores of expectation.

Fear takes an angry route,
striking everything in its path.

Shame hides in the gully at nightfall.

Love meets with the rich, mossy understory
of spores and seedlings –
fallen treasures from the last storm.

2

The hive buzz surges loud and clear.
Insistent voices clamor in agreement,
erupting with declarations
and assertions about "The Way."

Shrouded in my cloak of normalcy,
I'm made invisible by blending in.
I say what's expected
and nod when appropriate.

Living thus has turned into pretense.
But to what end?
I only have one…
…one life, that is.

But using my voice would surely rock the boat,
and I would be left bailing anyway.
My utterances would run counter to mainstream,
seeping through the fissures in my soul.

There's just so much noise out there –
a roiling cacophony of convention and certainty.
And to survive, I've made myself small on the outside,
shielding the inner waves that spin and swell.

There, idea fragments collect in small eddies.
Churning, they spit out the detritus,
and polished stones settle at the shorelines,
giving shape and substance to the water's edge.

Inside, I have more questions than answers.
Possibilities override certainties.
Wonderment surpasses assurance.
And emergence becomes the primary theme.

Though vanquished by the prevailing tides,
the buoyant dreams of my youth resurface and take hold.
Doesn't each voice carry equal merit?
Can't truth be heard in still waters?

3

Wake up! Something is happening here...now.
A surge of hope is unleashed in my soul,
breaking away from a deeply lodged tangle of angst,
and stunning me with its commanding radiance.

A gleeful squeal forms in the base of my throat.
I feel ready to leap out and play,
emerging from the protective shell I donned
in the face of all that passed before.

What a gift: finding hope in the rubble of death.

How?   HOW?

Casting aside the multilayered masks of resistance,
relinquishing the hard-edged certainty of knowing,
letting go of my carefully polished load,
I open my heart as life unfolds within me.

4

Deep diving is woven into the heart of my journey,
an inescapable free fall into the underworld.

Spiraling into the depth of a thing,
curving and spinning as the pressure builds,

I seek out the cavernous spaces,
where strange creatures lurk and treasures hide.

It's dark down here. Easy to get disoriented.
But wading around in the shallows was never my style.

I crave the nooks and crannies of the furrowed sea floor,
the barnacled underbelly of things long buried.

Such murky terrain marks the birthplace
of both beauty and pain, where the temperament of one is
equalized by the other.

Vertigo threatens as I prepare for decompression,
But gripping my anchor line, I test it for solidity.

Creatures of the deep encircle me, lending their support
as I seek passage into the full spectrum of life.

Submerged dreams join my buoyant ascent,
and I break the surface to a sun-glazed horizon.

5

My mind has been busy keeping secrets from my heart.
Not intentionally.
But there's that Gap. You know the one.
The Gap between when you know something,
and when you *know* it.

My mind fits comfortably around certain knowledge.
Assembling and assimilating without hesitation.
It's a lock down. Cut and dried.
Simply needs filing.

Emotional knowledge is craftier than that.
Elusive and slippery,
it would just as soon hide as be discovered.
In fact it seems to prefer hovering
at the very edge of consciousness.

Like Pleiades,
it goes invisible the minute I have it in my sights.
I try to creep up on it, but it refuses to be hunted.
It's not seeking my *discovery*.
Rather, it wants to *reveal* itself to me.

It has its own nature, its own clock,
and its own mysterious unfolding.
Bridging the Gap, I see now,
requires a shift in concentration:
A yielding. A welcoming stance.

As I pull my finger off the trigger of judgment,
and remove the scope of certainty,
grace saturates my peripheral vision,
and a fresh view spans the chasm.
A gentle stillness eclipses the horizon,
transforming certainty of the mind
into wonderment of the heart.

6

I have NOW, and aside from faith, speculation, or theory,
anything beyond that is unknowable.

Sitting with it,
I offer it my steady gaze of attention.

The whole shimmers and is briefly visible,
unadorned and nearly naked.

Though cloaked in the loveliest satin,
I see that it's marred by a newly apparent stain.

I begin to fidget in discomfort
and stare hard at the blemish.

Like a moth that's drawn to the flame,
I cleave to my earlier fallacy of perfection.

I long for the safe harbor of stasis
and the soothing illusion of constancy.

But life marches steadily onward,
and my lingering attention captures the motion.

Slowly, I see that the satin and the stain are the same,
and that their apparent duality unfolds along a spectrum.

What I thought of as solid
is itself in a state of emergence.

Steeling myself against the racing impulse to flee,
I rise above my fear of the unknown.

I enter the warm embrace of potentiality
and all the beauty *and* discomfort that entails.

7

Each thought is amplified by a chorus of notes,
pealing alternately with clarity and chaos.

Deciphering the melody requires stepping into the stream,
feeling the notes wash over the soul:
heart-beating rhythms of discovery,
hitching beats of confusion,
pulsing waves of sorrow,
and ecstatic notes of transformation.

Together, they weave the tapestry-like chords of life.

It's   all   one   song.

8

Raw, searing talons of grief rip through my soul,
engulfing me in their fiery embrace.

Dense smoke clouds my vision.
I gasp and find myself alone in a blizzard of sparks.

Scorched beyond recognition,
I scan my surroundings for anything familiar.

But all that was known is banished,
or burnished by the intensity of flames.

Shadowy shapes materialize in the darkness.
Shiny new markers herald the way.

I stagger forward and reach for them,
seeking comfort as I gain my bearings.

Finally, the blaze subsides, and I stumble into the clearing.
Looking behind, I see a trail of glowing embers.

9

Pruned my subconscious.
Discovered new shoots.

10

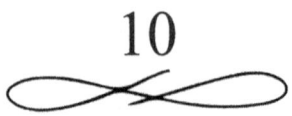

Pain surfaces and hovers at the door of awareness.
It squints in the morning light and gasps,
stunned at being out in the open after all this time.

The old darkness lay buried for decades,
shuttered in the cellar of my mind,
and rooted in the crushed hopes of my youth.

Echoes toll in cavernous hallways
as the ache tests its newfound freedom
and charts a shadowy course along the walls.

Meeting dawn as it bleeds through the curtains,
the exposed wound peels back layers of dust
and traces the outlines of my dreams.

Feathered fingers of faith drift along my thoughts,
slipping over the rim of consciousness,
and dusting the floorboards in downy tufts.

Suffused in light, the pain loosens its grip
and saunters over to an easy chair,
where it drapes itself against the soft fabric.

Comfortable now, relaxed even, its eyes meet mine,
and I see that it has all the room it ever needed.
Gracefully, it stretches, while transformation beckons.

11

Timeless, it speaks eternity.
It rises from the ashes of despair,
and embodies a full season of hope.
Born from pain and joy in equal measure,
It shimmers and becomes round.

12

Tendrils of hope curl along the fringes of my mind.
Wisps of smoldering hunger
light the chambers of my heart.

Each breath is singed with desire,
and senses awaken to the vibrational call of the universe:

Be.   Here.   Now.

Emergent potential sparks in each neuron,
seeking invitation in my dendritic embrace.

13

Something alive is growing in each of us…
touching everything we know,
turning roots to sawdust, and spinning flax to gold.
There's a path through all of it, a surety we must relax into.
Our individual and collective routes are now joined,
trailing ribbons across the sands of time.

14

Love's sap spills from the canopy of my soul
to the forest floor of my heart,
tracing the sweet veins of connection
from seedling to nurse log.

15

Your limber arms reach out to hold me with tender support.
Reading my fragility, you take care
with each gesture, every word.

I crouch, holding my guarded shell
with a learned readiness to recoil.

But your outstretched wings enfold me
with a knowing comfort,
and I lean into your steady embrace.

I breathe in your strength and make it my own.

16

A carefully constructed reserve
knits your brows and shields your heart,
as your lips slice through the concealing mask.

Our eyes focus and lock,
hearts beat in search of a unifying rhythm,
and your face dissolves into a million fragments.

Peace washes over us and hope beckons,
as your features transform,
re-assembling as Buddha.

17

My vision is clouded
with radiant wisps of crystalline cirrus
and a low-level fog of wonder.

18

Daubing a vibrant splash of sapphire on your temple,
I linger lovingly over the membrane
concealing your thoughts.

A full palette rests comfortably between us,
and we paint one other, venturing outside the lines
to coax shadowy images from the hidden contours,
where veiled forms shimmer beneath our skins.

Unaccountably, we recognize one another,
each canvas mirroring what we've longed to reveal.

This is no painting of material bodies…
it's an etching of our ethereal selves,
stretching far beyond the visible realm
into symbiotic connection of depth and light.

We move passionately now,
a profusion of color taking shape in multiple dimensions.

Awash in a suffusion of light, our spirits arc,
and saturated souls fuse in a surreal embrace,
where charged particles leap along the solar winds,
and orbital bodies collide in ecstatic release.

19

Galaxies of color flash behind my closed eyelids.
An expanding awareness takes root in my mind.
Unleashed hope saturates my spirit,
and an unaccountable energy possesses my limbs.
Starbursts tear through space to occupy my soul.

20

We only know
what we *know*
when we **know** it.

21

Windswept words race across thought clouds,
like a murder of crows.

22

A tidal arc of grief
rises in my heart,
flooding my veins with a crescendo of loss.

23

A tornado tears through the landscape of their minds.
They become paralyzed.

Despite the frenetic beating of their wings,
an infernal buzzing roars through their thoughts,
obstructing all meaning-making on the distorted horizon.

An exaggerated waving of her arms
accompanies each punctuated syllable,
and he's bewildered by the contortions of her face.

His mouth moves and a torrent of words
rush through the opening.
Unfathomable! A vexing dissonance
for all the sense she can make of it.

Stooped by the weight of their worries,
they cling to their descending chords.
The shrill notes of fear mute their capacities for listening.
And the harsh tones of despair
clog their filters of understanding.

They stand motionless amidst the rubble of their resistance.

Stony silences rattle their nerves,
and frayed vibrations wrack their bodies.

Aside from their rigid stance, everything else is in motion.

This awareness slips silently
under the door of consciousness – whispering,
"wake up…this too shall pass…all is not lost."

24

I'm thrown against the chiseled shell of my original wound
as new triggers amplify a primal pain.

Fanged blades of fear threaten my equilibrium
in throaty gusts of reverberation.

I struggle to right myself
and gain ground as I reach into my soul.

Clutching handfuls of hope,
I remember that I've survived this and more before.

25

A squadron of memories stirs the roof of her consciousness
A question mark furrows her brow
Her lips arch downward in disbelief,
and her jaw tightens in clenched restraint
She trains her eyes to still the dam of tears.
Ripped asunder, her heart falls from her chest,
and blood pools at her feet.
She is powerless to stem the flow.

26

Scalded by the blistering shrapnel of love,
buried under a raging storm of angst,
seared by the acrid smoke of fury,
her heart is scorched beyond all recognition.

27

Resistance cinches me into a suit of suffering,
where clanging armor shutters my heart.
Encased in this stifling universe,
my screams ricochet along the seams.

28

The raging noise in my head subsides
as the rolling silence swells between us.

It crashes on the shores of withholding,
cresting in foamy resistance,
where resolve meets a daunting series of waves,
and we become ensnared in the murky undertow –
only to find ourselves co-conspirators
with the secrets of these depths.

Speaking to you now might carry us toward the surface.
But whether articulation would send us ashore
or convey us out to sea
remains as unformed
as the drop of a single sound in an ocean of words.

29

Voodoo demons come a-knockin' at the door,
rattling my cage, makin' my spirit sore.

I'm lookin' for my armor in the face of all this fear.
Feel I'm under siege with everything I hold dear.

But it's not the time for walls
That'd only keep my spirit small.

It's a time for reaching higher,
and settin' those walls on fire.

To burn those demons down,
burn 'em all the way to the ground

And make myself loom large,
takin' up the whole of my heart.

It's the only path through,
and nothing else is gonna do.
Certainly the only way…the only way back to you.

30

Speeding thoughts race across my crowded mind,
etching furrowed tunnels in their haste.

I still my focus to that deep inner voice,
and make meaning out of the commotion.

31

The stillness of one's spirit
yields hints of the unknowable...
lends texture to the invisible.

32

Kneeling at the altar of trust,
intention begets understanding,
and bears the fruit of compassion.

33

An unaccountable umbrella of trust
encircles our hearts as the rain falls.

34

Following my mind into my mind,
I try to decipher what condition my condition is in…
and sequester myself there,
where eddies and currents drag me down, down.

Submerged in the murky depths,
I spin, tumble, and reach out,
striving to break free
from the centripetal force.

I see a light at the surface
and reach for it with desperate recognition.
It is me – adrift, untethered, and alive.
I float up into myself.

35

Footsteps through the heart
wind precipitously along the narrowest of paths.

Often treacherous, and oh so slippery,
the route commands my careful attention.

My concentration yields the richest of fortunes:
a curtain of sunbeams along the meandering route.

36

Dawn envelopes me in the lush dewy grasses of youth
when the eerie notes of the varied thrush
slip into my dreams and summon my awareness.

Fog stretches in billowy tents
and seeps across the valley floor.
I inhale, breathing in possibility and hope.

37

Detached from neural reckoning
unhinged from psychic reasoning
the mind elopes with the heart
in playful pursuit and perpetual folly.

38

She harvested a profusion of words
as they ripened in her soul.

www.ingramcontent.com/pod-product-compliance
Lightning Source LLC
Chambersburg PA
CBHW051719040426
42446CB00008B/965